L

LANDLOCKED

Mark Ford

For Hugh

'Let us go now, you and I...'

with all best wishes,

Mark

Chatto & Windus
LONDON

25/11/10

Published in 1992 by
Chatto & Windus Ltd
20 Vauxhall Bridge Road
London SW1V 2SA

A CIP catalogue record for this book is available
from the British Library

ISBN 0 7011 3750 9

Copyright © Mark Ford 1992

Reprinted 1998

Mark Ford has asserted his right to be
identified as the author of this work.

Photoset by
Cambridge Composing (UK) Ltd
Cambridge

Printed in Great Britain
by Mackays of Chatham PLC,
Chatham, Kent.

Acknowledgements

Acknowledgements are due to the editors of the following publications, in which some of these poems first appeared:

Literary Review, London Magazine, The London Review of Books, The New Statesman, North Magazine, Oxford Poetry, Poetry Review, Soho Square 1, The Times Literary Supplement, Verse.

Fifteen of these poems were published in *New Chatto Poets II* (1988).

Contents

Passion Play   3

If You Could Only See Me Now!   4

Christmas   5

Landlocked   7

Street Violence   8

General Knowledge   9

Stocking Up   10

Night Out   11

My Shoulder-Length Hair   13

Consumer Durables   14

Invisible Assets   15

Daily   16

Winter Underwear   17

I'm   18

Free the Spirit   19

Snowfall   20

Course Adjustment   23

Second-Hand Clothes   24

Unpicking the Knot   25

A Head for Heights   26

The Queer Smell of Gas   27

Policing Beaconsfield   28

Sneaker Dot-to-Dot   29

Soft Sift   30

Coastal   31

Affirmative Action   32

A Close Friend   33

In the Adirondacks   34

High Performance   35

A Swimming-Pool Full of Peanuts   36

Cross-Section   39

Kid Crazy   40

Super Black Thursday   41

Demise   42

Then She Said She Had to Go   43

Funny Peculiar   44

Last to Leave   45

Manifest Destiny   46

Chattering Teeth   47

Under the Bridge   48

Resting Up   49

Ledgers   50

Outing   51

For Xanthe Gresham

O grant that like to Peter I
May like to Peter B.
And tell me lovely Jesus Y
Old Jonah went to C.

John Keats

LANDLOCKED

PASSION PLAY

Can we hear you Bury? Noooeoooe!
Your tide is out
And drift-wood fires our cause.
We chip the keeper, and ram the ball home.

Our bicycle has been stolen. Thieves
Came in the night and took it;
Now I'm tanked up, and celebrating.
We chip the keeper, and ram the ball home.

To be sleepless on a starless night
In Croydon, begets a sound defence,
And vicious attack. Why lie? you wearily inquire.
We chip the keeper, and ram the ball home.

IF YOU COULD ONLY SEE ME NOW!

When I'm in power I will pursue landlords
across the country. Right now, life
has me boxed in, and my cries for help drift inscrutably
around willows, oak trees, and grief-stricken elms.
I left home young, and since then I've roamed
and roamed, following my nose, through deserts and
    cities,
always alone, in forests, living in trees –
What a life!
           They say every character is complex
but I am tangled up like spaghetti; I lie here, observing
    the stars,
a stiffening breeze tickling my feet, my pillow
a petrified log. The birds chirruping in the early dawn
ignore me, while I dream I am a lunatic, striding the land,
scattering seed and crushing the asphodel
beneath my pitiless heel;
but finally the day arrives,
bursting softly over the horizon.
                      For the West
has been ruined. You left under a cloud
but I love you. If you could only see me
now! I stand here, incompetent,
tracing figures on a map, fully dressed
as if it were already evening, enraged
and impenitent, clenching my teeth.

CHRISTMAS

I very much enjoyed your latest book I lied having
NOT read it. Hurrah! We're all of us bright as chickens
As if Jack liked Chrissie and Chrissie liked Jack.
Ah, we had a good season, then, we drew all five fixtures!
For Christmas, I asked my mother to knit me a tie
To go with my tunic. No! she snapped,
Go out and buy one. So off I samba –
When it was Sunday and all the shops were shut –
The streets are full enough though and there are
Some fine ankles showing through – my fertile
    imagination! –
I see mini-skirts where others see only galoshes,
I can count all my exes at the bus stop
All over with tinsel, polluting the atmosphere with
Their dirty breaths. It is lunch-time
So I hail a friend munching a pastrami sandwich –
He spotted me and then he lay flat in the snow.
'Stop playing hookey,' I yelled, 'You're grown up now!'
Then I thought – but what if something is really wrong?
I screeched to a halt beside his head
The snow spooning up into my sandals, and I shouted
'Get up, Jake,' and I toed him. Any moment
I expect him to grab me playfully by the ankle,
I quite liked the idea of a tussle in the Christmas snow
On Main Street. He didn't budge though.
Only the yellow stains of the mustard from his sandwich
    drooled
Scenting the crisp air. 'Ah, come on Jake,
You think this a rodeo?' I whisper to him,
'Why not get up?' And I threaten him with
The police, arrest, his sister in tears on the phone.
And I poured hot coffee down his throat, murmuring
'But it's the season of Goodwill, no one plays for keeps
Over Christmas.' What kept him down there,
Face in the slush, people must've seen him eating

Pastrami sandwiches before?
                                Apparently not. I waited
All afternoon by him, chain-smoking his Camels,
And then I watched his feet disappear into the ambulance
That arrived after dark. I stamped his damp sandwich
Back into the snow. People, I thought,
Will find this when the thaw sets in
And wonder about it, shopping or on their way to work,
Birds like sparrows will nibble the sesame seeds
And wish it were Pumpernickel,
It will liven up their Easter.

LANDLOCKED

See, no hands! she cried
Sailing down the turnpike,
And flapped her arms like a pigeon,
And from the backseat Solomon, her spaniel, answered
  her
By woofing ever more madly at each passing car!
What a trek it was out west
And back again! Weeks on end she spent
Stranded in the worst motels, poor thing,
Could never quite make up her mind to go on
To go back, to stay absolutely where she was.
Such awful doubts assailed her in the prairie states –
For days she chewed her favourite gum on the hard
  shoulder
And whispered her difficult secrets to the wheat
Where game Solomon yelped, and, true to form,
The unmiraculous wheat only rustled through its rosary
  once more.
She sent me a postcard from somewhere
In Missouri, and then again from Amarillo,
Texas. She said she thought she'd make it
All the way to sunshine California, but she said
She couldn't promise she'd like it when she did
Or even that she'd get all the way over to the ocean there,
Which didn't surprise me or disappoint me one little bit,
And I sent one back to an address in Vegas saying,
Well why should you, unless of course you want to?

STREET VIOLENCE

I asked for nothing better than a five-spot.
I thought that modest. Whisking around
On her single stiletto, though, her lips twitching,
She stared me in the eye so forcefully
I saw at once only the familiar words –
Nothing Doing. I determined there and then
To take each disappointment as best I could.
There you have it, once we were so close
Nothing short of a machete
Could have separated us. Now . . .
I watched her hail a shiny yellow taxi.
It was such a wonderful afternoon!
I moved off down the block, my block,
Its bright red bricks seemed to watch me,
There was a sudden breeze fresh in my face
And the sun was so strong it made my eyes water.
Too bad, I thought, for her sake,
That she didn't remember me like she should have.

GENERAL KNOWLEDGE

Atlanta emerged from the ribbed red soil
Of Georgia; it now has
One of the busiest airports in America.

From there we flew to the cradling arms
Of New Orleans; here, where the Mississippi
Ends, perspiring jazz musicians like bulls lock horns.

It's said that every forty minutes the world is girdled
By a satellite; with a nail I trace the thin blue
Veins of the delta winding dubiously towards the sea.

STOCKING UP

No one lives in the imagination, or if they do
they probably stink of garlic. What a thought!
Five o'clock. Everyone's pushing off to the country for
   the weekend.
What a jamboree the streets enjoy, sticky
traffic jams, spouting hydrants, and roofs that catch the
   red and dying sun.
While Tom Cat plays with baby, there's mother
waving us farewell. 'Drive carefully,' she cries
as we pull out, 'It's Friday night, remember.'
We slide so easily though through strings of amber traffic
   lights
on our smooth journey to the shops, our windows rolled
   down
all the way. The light
lies down beautifully over the new arcade.
What a lovely evening! My trolley is overflowing
with supplies. In the low flat sweep of store window
my friends and I see ourselves reflected.
The lot behind us is beginning to fill up,
could be they'll introduce valet parking at some point.
   Pleased,
we fill up the trunk and go back for more
('You again' the cash girl joked us)
enough to feed us and our families for
a part, at least, of the long hot summer now approaching.

NIGHT OUT

The grandest illusion was one Saturday night
after a sleepy sleepless week, having left the spadework
mainly until the weekend, we thought we'd go anyway
so sitting there in the dark, the same old flickering
black and white black and white the old phono too
until the escape scene when everybody conceived the
    worst
the most tremendous head-aches, forget about the Alps,
where's the nearest aspirin store, so that, temporarily,
    was it
no one attempts a pass like that without a technician!
Anyway, that night was the worst of all, the flutes
still going in my head, needless to say I couldn't sleep,
I hated to think of them stuck not quite over
the border, without the cow, or Lotte, dumb dumb
dumb, unfair, so I sneaked back out of the dorm, it was
still drizzling a bit, another grey night, the same one,
and I hooded and winked the porter, just as he was
    locking up,
cool as you please, an old trick from my circus days,
    barefoot
though, all in my pyjamas, I crawled like a marine
through three layers of books, swung manfully around
the balconies only my dressing-gown cord between me
    and
plunging twenty-five feet into a beckoning court-yard
until, elbows working, I inched into the auditorium,
lights down, not a sound, and I went over the projection
    room
with a fine tooth-comb, till I found it and slipped it on
the last reel and played it now to my own satisfaction.
I wouldn't deny it was spooky enough all alone there
in the dark, just the old black and white, and
the volume control was all whizzy, now loud now soft
and not quite in time, and I was nervous enough too

any time expecting the familiar clap on the shoulder, it
came, what's going on then, kicking and screaming
let me see the end, did they make it, I can't remember
if they make it, on deaf ears it falls, so
I'm gagged and spend a night in the slammer very
     romantic
and am arraigned on various charges, my character
generally impugned, and I never think I'll get
to see the inside of a P.O.W. camp again in *this* world!
I was let out alright, though, the principal stood up for
     me,
my record was good, though I wish he hadn't, I felt
like a cockroach having breakfast with him and
his wife a certain Sunday later in the month
no explanations asked only how were my poor parents,
     bearing up,
what a shame I gave up racket-ball, someone
was on a winning streak as usual, the eggs that morning
were bitter in my mouth. At last it all quieted down,
as I knew it would, who after all could care less
except me who cares less, I care less than any and all of
     you,
it's a major strength of my character, I care less
and less, and of course will never but never give that up.

MY SHOULDER-LENGTH HAIR

It can usually be done
with a telephone call
or other evidence, within the slow
drip of time, or even when
it's threatening to burst its banks!
The testy voice will recall
its mother, such and such dream sequences,
long love prayers, and their mannerisms –
and awkwardnesses – *Touché*.
a-e-i-o-u – oh the lost art of
being tuneful . . . the microphone
stutters, respecting the paintwork,
and the unhung curtains, and general
disorder, and the angry young
mattress nailed to the floor.

CONSUMER DURABLES

Our last trip together
Had all the ingredients of disaster: you
In satin de Chine flounces, trimmed with lace,
And topped by three tiers of head-gear sporting fake,
   colourful birds
In the act of perching; for myself
A heavy smile, a devoted laugh,
Jokes and anecdotes beyond belief . . .

Sometimes I 'want' poetry
As a man wants a woman, or a brave his squaw.
The sea clutches its single pebbles to its breast,
A packet on the misty grey horizon,
The time almost four o'clock. For hours
I've watched these bare-assed
Men, women, and children, ecstatic in their doings,
I can feel the tingle of the sun myself
As I make my way back to my shore-side condominium.

And then the approach of evening
Is like stepping into space. The clanking machinery
Of the ferris wheel rumbles beneath each thought,
As we dawdle around the shies, and pop-gun ranges,
Though our easy chairs beckon. You beg a ride on
   anything
But I refuse. Beneath the shadows
Of the outhouses I ate the last lozenge
And ground the empty packet
Back into the sod with my heel.

INVISIBLE ASSETS

After he threw her through a
plate-glass window, nature seemed that much closer.

Even the dastardly divisions in society
might be healed by a first-rate glazier.

Of course, on Sundays families still picnicked
boldly on the village green, and afterwards

marvelled at the blacksmith's glowing forge –
how strong they all were in those days!

And yet how small! Even a man only six foot tall
was then esteemed a veritable giant.

Surely the current furore over architecture
would have evoked from them only pitying smiles.

Meanwhile, the market for landscapes has never
been firmer. This view, for instance, includes

seven counties, and a bull charging around in its
    paddock.

DAILY

Newspaper clippings drift
across the Walworth Road,
and, in the unmentionable cold, the shops
incline their shutters. I imagine
chalk dinosaurs erupting from the doorways,
and a tinkle of glass to accompany
the carefree motion of their scaly tails . . .

Inside the soup
has already congealed inside the single pan
around whose rim moss sprouts,
and released into the air the innumerable sightless
    microbes
that will later perplex the authorities.
Hungry pets yelp in locked attics, while we gawp
as at last the rubbish enters the furnace.
Turn out the light – some story
is breaking, crumbling, collapsing
under the intolerable weight of fresh evidence
whispered over telephones and hedges: awful
types prosper and suddenly the rhumba
is everywhere the rage again, a perfect dance
for couples or singles, for either in front
of the mirror or actually on the crowded dance-floor.

WINTER UNDERWEAR

How vividly the football flew
Only he would remember;
And likewise the dark purple scarves
In which the body was later wound.

Until one day speech
Is merely syntax, and one's head
Is so full of stratagems
The tea freezes solid in its pot;

And a fresh snow covers the plains
Above which newfangled aircraft constantly
Manoeuvre, their vapour trails soft
And brilliant as the white

Winter underwear she is even now pulling on.

I'M

I'm an aggressive man
Always walking up escalators
And sniffing out rights. Sharks
Infest our local waters,
You too I despise.
                Night floods the land.
We must leave now. Armies of flowers
Advance, stealing the oxygen
Right out of our mouths.

FREE THE SPIRIT

So polite he could almost have been
The villain in a Charlotte Brontë novel –

If only he knew what we were about to do!
A school bell rings shrilly in the distance

And the very seconds prepare to choke
On their own significance, marked out by an orange
   kitchen clock.

Noon arrives nursing its own peculiar threats;
No wind and a soft miaowing sound

Accompany the last hopes of the vanishing day, and soon
It will be more than late enough for a drink.

Leaving, on the other hand, would mean
Forking out for a new hair-cut, and arguing

The whole thing through with the face man again.

SNOWFALL

You must be snug in there
you and your seventh TV wife
with a cat and a fire, I swear
I'm so glad you ended up with that.

He writes! How wonderful. And
bloodies his own nails and nose
for sensation. He has a firm hand-
shake, why I'm glad of their liaison.

And she sweet vague snowdrop
is also carefully posed each morning. Does he
draw her? They sketch each other! And what could stop
her melting but amnesia?

I've a new taste in my mouth all day.
It rises overnight and hangs there,
and chokes my breath, all morning I say
this final straw, now chew it over . . . please.

My system! I fiddle while Rome burns. But find
another, or more untrampled snow
which doesn't exist. Kind kind
rain has pockmarked everything.

In the afternoon I swept
the porch and yard and dressed. We left
in the early evening, under grey skies, the car leapt
into life, and I relaxed with a sigh into its rich upholstery.

Hush! my mother said . . . The lights
are green but she won't go.
Move! mother, I said, nights
are long on the Pulaski skyway.

We shunt around town for hours.
Ah, mother, she must have been held up,
her car wouldn't start! Even ours
is unsafe in this blizzard.

Oh mother, I'm sorry. Let's go,
we'll go home. Don't say anything,
please, I wish we didn't know
each other so well, drive safely.

We stare out the car.
The snow is rain for a while
and then slush. I find where we are
on the map. Mother is silent while she drives.

And it is silence which falls
with more snow. I don't care, I must speculate.
Mother ignores my silence and calls
the weather awful when at last we pull over.

My dear girl! My sweet friend!
I compose to you in the hissing dark,
you are a poker-player to the end,
your breasts are mushrooms without stems . . .

We try the engine again.
It coughs but it is frozen and out
of gas. I see the shapes of moving men
blanket the windows, they rattle the fender.

Mother! Ghosts! She finds an old
tartan travelling rug and lies down in
the back. Get some sleep, I am told.
Her breathing goes quiet and regular.

No ghosts. I can conjure up though
wide-eyed fevers to sweep the nation and
bloody betrayals and grotesque obesities and low
heaps of wrecked trucks and other violence.

What I picture comes true – their livestock frozen in the
   snow
and polar bears in our once warm houses
and the creaking of glaciers and a wild ice-floe
and death and flames in the desperate cold.

Only once during the night I tried the radio,
it was dead, and once I dreamed I was on the phone
to my sweetheart. Believe me, I said, I can't just go,
with the frostbite I've got, and hush my mother's still
   sleeping.

COURSE ADJUSTMENT

Language *is* life (God help us)
it's more like a vinegar eye-bath to me.
Another semester. CJ and the committee
are at each other's throats again. It takes him a week
to unclench his fist after each session.
I can't help adding my penny's worth.
What does the doc say? The doc's out fishing
and advises you to join him. Picture it,
out there, in the icy stream, the water just
creeping over your waders – go ahead,
it's yours for the asking – whatever you catch
you get to eat. 'Nature's lightning's been known
to strike even her firmest favourites once,' I end up
  warning him,
but it's the bull-headed people who always
get their own way. My Ten Commandments were struck
  clean
from the curriculum. All the core courses
were overhauled, now I drum my fingers
on the lectern airily, but
with a huge frog croaking in my throat.

SECOND-HAND CLOTHES

More than a familiar face, I knew him when young,
And now the world is his ante-room.
We're overrun by ancestors and associates, well-wishers
    from everywhere,
As we ponder the exact wording of these huge banners
Tacked out for our consideration . . .

                                        yet meanwhile,
    still unseen,
You must watch the waxy telephone cradled between
Her anxious ear and suspicious mouth. And truly,
Her wary voice begins, truly typical scheduling begins
    here –
You and I are involved, though I contemplate marriage
    no longer.

I have fought for this, on billowing office
Furniture, my trouser creases indistinguishable in the
    gloom
Of early winter, and pitilessly exposed by sharp
    fluorescent spring.
My letter of 12th August remains unanswered
And perhaps unopened on your desk, yet still
The billboards flicker, and I feel a rough hand
Flex, and prepare, somewhere in the vicinity of my
    shoulder

UNPICKING THE KNOT

Pot plants unwatered on the sun-deck
Like moaning minnies lie down and die.

Her lips have twisted into a random smile, but
In her mind she curses in her mother tongue.

The room is now an inverted fish tank;
Things float helplessly up towards the glass –

Her brushes, her combs, her trash,
Objects it were useless even to list.

Each noise fades away like forgotten
Sex, its stripes etched faintly on the buzzing air.

You dream of a crisp welcome, leading into some
Precise business proposals. A three-course

Luncheon will follow shortly after.

A HEAD FOR HEIGHTS

Therefore a host of madmen
Have grown to love this sunny spot
And the expansive view of the city it affords.
While I clatter shut the lid of our faded
Lunch-box, you shelter your eyes from the dazzling
   horizon
That surrounds us, sprinkled with trees
And speeding towards us and the magnificent city
Spread out for us, like a map, on the brown
Bumpy plain at our feet.

But where do they come from
These early voyagers of spring, hushed
And stricken and camouflaged among the waving trees?
No one knows. And the gathering roar of exploding
   leaves
One hears behind them, in contrast, the sap
And hidden movements, brand us
Conclusively, I think; the rustling forest
Must provide fruit, and quiet pools for bathing.
But leaving aside this, how awkwardly you move,
My dear, forgetting my companion must be spryer
Than any monkey, with limbs immaculate, and a walker
Of great distances, and that day and night
You must continually seek to astonish me
With your vital gift for life.

THE QUEER SMELL OF GAS

The grey of 3 AM envelops her room again. Hush!
From its mountainous source the Thames
Inches its way towards Southend
Under a glaring, three-quarters moon.

To grasp more fully his insignificance
Man propounds new and ever stranger theories
Of language and evolution. Others object merely
That the sexual revolution has been betrayed.

The day after the deal, the TV off, I took up
My woods, remembering Finsbury Circus.
The will was not to be contested. In theory
All the chairs in this house are now solely mine to dispose
   of.

POLICING BEACONSFIELD

He talks with his feet;
'Er – ,' he pauses before replying.

Two pale fish flap
Through the aquarium.

How often did he take
Mind-expanding drugs?

A twist of cirrus, drifting slowly
Across the white ridge.

She lies there unmoving;
Her straw, they think, needs changing.

We voters long to be abused.
We love the truly merciless decisions.

SNEAKER DOT-TO-DOT

excitement, with the bit of a bore and I each glimpsing
    each other's purely imaginative vegetation,
that is, with our own two eye-pieces, up and down, there
    being no way out of here while the night watch
grins and stares so. At last we lay beneath dowdy green
    skies, then off
to be touched by some arch-fiend's idea of a typical,
    well-equipped extravaganza, high broody clouds
    in the distance,
but too airy, too like collapse.

relaxing, with extra-hard idleness, dimmed night-shades,
    rare phosphor
explosions, and the raw earth lapping the corrugated
    walls of the hut. Just
hark at the night-jar, consider the machine-worker,
    search for corrosion. Rat-
a-tat-tat small fire clashes with the boom of heavy
    artillery, I take out my
gleaming silver sword, my grandfather's, and polish it.

sleep, the fire crackles according to its own sweet will.
    Why feed it? For
the sake of the dry life, sweet temperance forever! Red
    swing doors open on the empty
cabaret and reveal my singer and her duck-backed
    manager. It's she who with firm dislike sinks
lifeless in my arms each night, until I console her – with
    the news, with money, and with the wild stories
with which I interpret her dreams.

SOFT SIFT

A chill March wind blows through
The vogue for cultural references;
In a twist the sporting chance we momentarily
Enjoyed is shut up like a geometry box.

Even the trees groan at the thought of standing
The test of time. Already a new challenger
Spars for an opening, the co-ordinates slide around
Like the proverbial vole in an hour-glass.

And now beneath my cummerbund I feel
The familiar drain through the glands to the various pits.
I have etched kohl above my eyelashes.
Somewhere there is a problem, a rain-streaked mangle

Waiting in some yard for its unlikely delivery.

COASTAL

From afar I saw where we were
And how his predilections had changed
On the hills, the grey sea, and the rocks.
And from this you see, how, when I move
Through the thinning air, I take note, and follow
Like a pup, obedient on the sand . . .

                                            Now
The lovely clapboard fades, the abandoned coves
And fishing smacks, and I can feel the dirtiness
Like gold thick on my palm, the rubbish
I shift into the piles at which I stare.

AFFIRMATIVE ACTION

In the original raree-show, of which this is a pale
Imitation, phantoms swore and hurled mountains at each
   other;

Tiny, endless columns of red-jacketed soldiers
Adjusted their busbys before attacking a farmhouse;

And 'White Light/White Heat' blared
From bank upon bank of shuddering loudspeakers.

Now a vast customer complaints department
Imposes everywhere its blinkered theories of art.

Come on, Government! You're supposed to be in charge!
What about these here hooligans running naked through
   the streets?

What about the stream winding through pleasant
   meadows
And the cows brooding in the grass?

What about midges, and toffee-apple, and washing days?

A CLOSE FRIEND

She thought it might be vitamins.
I thought, rather, here was a man
Determined to waste his life.
We met in a bar to discuss tactics.
'He's alright,' she declared in a whisper,
'Quite brilliant often.' I asked her what she thought
Of his prospects. 'Qu-qu-qu-quite good,'
She said. 'Oh no!' I said,
'Don't tell me you've picked up his stutter!'

IN THE ADIRONDACKS

Bumbling with a jackass hair-cut through the stormy
  weather
With my two companions, both fresh and witty – after a
  while
We were introduced, formally, and after that I enticed
  them on
With promises of extra time. Our two bloods fought,
The bloods of moraine and of ether, admiring the
  prospect
Exactly where the heavy snow covered the peaks and
  valleys, and lay waiting
For my perspiring friends to relax, and call for a new
  enterprise, a halt, an explanation,
Or indeed for me to kick their stubborn behinds . . .
I thought – like a thorn – here is my weary foot thudding
  through
Their winter padding, its neat quilts and roughened oil-
  skins,
Fierce with exhaustion and contempt! I ripped
The gaudy strings of pearls from around their necks.
I derived no solace from stripping their mounted layers of
  clothing
Nor from exposing their healthy bodies to the wind.
Now, as I write, with my own pen, wifeless, rich and
  comfortable,
With how little pleasure do I recall that disastrous
  vacation in the Adirondacks.

HIGH PERFORMANCE

Seaweed drips from one's head
Looking like hair – only green, straggling,
And with innumerable pods to pop.

Together we wander on through this literary-critical
Conundrum. We've spoken of it before
And have agreed we'd die for less.

It's all in the name of 'high performance',
Which really means good looks, a super intelligence,
And one of those tight-fitting, wavy-patterned sweaters.

A SWIMMING-POOL FULL OF PEANUTS

A stifling blanket day out west I was working the desert
   states
nothing for days thank-you ma'm door slams in my face
   (again)
so I mosey out round the back where my vehicle sits
   melting I'll
just check the set-up the outhouses the grass is all stiff
and plastic the trees are all lifeless and there's no shade
nothing stirring until I come across right in the open
a whole swimming-pool full of peanuts I think
I've gone mad so I shut my eyes and I count
to five and look again and they're still resting there
very quietly an inch or so I suppose below
the high-water mark they're a light tan colour
and the tiles around are a lovely cool aqua-blue
only there's no water just these peanuts.
Well this is a hoax I can tell some monkey's idea
of a good joke for who'd fill up a fair-sized swimming-
pool entirely with peanuts unless they're painted in
which case it's a nice piece of work so I
kneel down in my best suit on the edge
(tie at half-mast because of the heat)
and with a loud snigger I dip in my finger
just to see it sinks into small grainy nuggets
sand-coated and a bit greasy some whole some in
half I draw it out and examine it all shiny with oil
the nail gleaming and I lick it to find out the taste
SALT! madness! the genuine article! straight salted
   peanuts!
this gets me because what kind of mad case goes
to the trouble of building a swimming-pool and then fills
   it
instead of with water with salted peanuts right up to the
   brim
I'm the butt of his jest this goop is taking the michael

almost physically I can feel him pulling my leg so
I lean over again and lower my head carefully until my
left eye is level with the glistening expanse for no
reason I'm feeling all queasy this pool full of peanuts
is disturbing my eye won't focus in case in an instant
they turn into piranha fish and green mambas
or anything else that might be hiding down there.

Still nothing moved I admit it was quiet too quiet
all I could hear was my own labouring breath
so in both clammy hands I scoop up fistful after fistful
and I watch them trickle through my fingers and glitter in
the sun I go back to my car and open up the trunk
I take out my golf-bag I select a nine-iron
and without a thought for my own safety I head back
to the pool and I swing away reckless in that peanut
    bunker
I scatter peanuts like a madman all over around there
they go flying like sand-flies in all directions like golf-
balls they arc away and shower down like buff-coloured
    hail
and I thresh and flail like one possessed
but nothing is uncovered it's no good from the edge
so feet first I leap in at the deep end
brandishing my golf-club and hit away
like a good soldier but there's more and more always
though I swing a good hour at the end of that
I am exhausted and my skin itches from the salt
and my clothes are all clinging I collapse in the middle
buoyed up by the peanuts the whole thing is hopeless
my pores are all clogged so I say let sleeping dogs lie
and I crawl to the side and haul myself out and
shake out the loose peanuts from the creases of my suit
I pick them out of my socks and empty out my shoes
I brush them out of my armpits and angrily I throw
my nine-iron into the middle of the pool where it sinks
without trace and I storm back to my car and

I make this resolution never ever if you can ever avoid it
fool around with a swimming-pool like this one
well a swimming-pool full of peanuts is not worth the
  trouble.

CROSS-SECTION

We all knew of his exploits –
The flowers from the Dean's wife for his overhead,
The chair carved into an oak tree bearing his name,
And the day he passed his driving test
Wine in hall for all.
                              A songster
Left out in the rain trills bleakly
It's morning: new habits for me too,
Sawing things palely in half on my saw-horse
Each Sunday afternoon.

KID CRAZY

Rangers patrol these woods. Orange discs
Mark their favourite trees, by which
They lie, between roots smothered in moss.

Each visitor takes home a scrap
Of bark. Their names
Are entered in the way-station's register.

Supplies must be hauled in
By especially bred pack-horse
Across a treacherously cratered terrain.

When a gaucho mops his brow with the hem
Of his singlet, all eyes seek out
The source of his implacable tattoos.

SUPER BLACK THURSDAY

Intense pressure builds up
In the sinus, making the legs
Weightless, the eyes water.
Beside me my mug, enamelled,
With its slogan; its star-signs
In tea-leaves.
          The screen's blip
Has all but vanished. Green graphics
Reveal all – how here I wept,
There you scratched yourself,
On this estate I grew up, denting the garage doors
With my ball.
            PM. The newcomer's swivel chair
Lolls empty: across the city
Terminals are ablaze with the absurd news,
The markets shooting out in all directions,
In random, jagged leaps. Your eyes are
Seized by dysfunction. Then on this
Super day we gathered together, shouting,
Drank beer in flocks, somehow wheeled home
Reeling with it, breathing it all in, the night,
The ghostly carriage cloth, the stations blurred
And moving, always moving.

DEMISE

Rodents swarm over the earth; even Natty
Bumppo is taken aback. Scrambling eggs
Or brewing up porridge, he angles
The pan crazily over the fire.

Why bother to know about anything
Except the signs of the forest? Hark!
A Mingo moves stealthily on his custom-built
Moccasins from bush to bush.

Are we all thus accursed? The muzzle
Of *La Longue Carabine* pokes
Through the foliage; the sun gleams
On the frontiersman's mouse-coloured rifle.

THEN SHE SAID SHE HAD TO GO

The drawing-room was full.   The commuters half-turned
    At last the angry hostess   to wave good-bye to
        approached and   their friends. About their
            whispered   feet fell the
                black   words
                into my   of their
        unsuspecting ear.   evening newspapers.

            My new cow   Lunch is a strange experience
    is loose in the field.   here. The big hall is
        With her tail she   full of birds
                swishes   swooping around –
                    away   flies
        and wanders   a carrot I
off happily to the fence.   was about to eat.

        A large sea swell   The desk was littered
    swamped the bay;   with books. She banged
        the streets were   the front door, and I tried
            drenched, and   to imagine
                    salt   water
            was found as   flowing
far inland as Newton.   from her lovely eyes.

FUNNY PECULIAR

I sit down here drinking hemlock
While terrible things go on upstairs.

Sweat creeps like moss outward to the palms,
And time itself now seems a strange, gauze-like medium.

Sleep will leave still newer scars each night, or,
Infuriatingly, is a curtain that refuses to close.

On the horizon, bizarre consolations make themselves
Known – a full fridge, a silent telephone,

The television quiet in its corner.
Everything and nothing have become a circular

Geometrical figure, seamlessly joined,
To be wrestled innocently this way and that

Into the most peculiar almost whimsical shapes.

LAST TO LEAVE

Things not necessarily funny
will stick in the memory, like recipes
for success, or how one once stood up
laughing, happy, a chip off the old block;
and I too, some days, rise, the applause
of the dying committee still ringing in my ears,
addressing absent friends, and those present,
for better or for worse, the tears now pouring
openly down my ravaged face. It's as if
our spirits merge, and the collection plates are
overflowing into the last few minutes
of the time remaining, as unknown guests
prowl through the empty bedrooms searching
for the stoles, fur hats, and winter coats
they deposited somewhere earlier in the evening.

MANIFEST DESTINY

Apologies are for the birds.
The only way out is down
Through the earth – hence the slight
Squint and the furred paws like a mole's.

You meanwhile are immersed
In your bubble-bath. Minor aches and pains
Dissolve in the soothing aromatic foam. Steam
Mists over the bathroom's several mirrors.

Like a trapper the spirit of freedom
Stalks the land. Already the generous
Pioneers respond with small cries, and
Tears, and heated haggling over suitcases.

CHATTERING TEETH

My teeth may chatter
But how I love her.
On frosty nights her silhouette
Dances against the brown barn door
Mocking me for something I might have said to her
During the day.
I follow the glittering points of the moon
Caught in her eyes,
Weaving towards me where I lie in the hay
Amazed at her dark moving arms
When all else is quiet asleep,
Only she in the silence
Flinging her legs in random cartwheels,
I hear clearly the touch of her bare feet
In the straw, lightly pressing the wooden boards . . .

But by dawn the stars are fading, and the dray
Is restless, wanting attention.
Such weather we're having, it won't last,
I remark outloud to myself, shivering, and watching
The sky, and imagining snow
Descending from it like a blanket,
Drift upon drift, piling up
Like a dome, around the various doors,
The roof, the attic window . . .

UNDER THE BRIDGE

A secret fund of rage
Frees him from all worldly obligations.
He casts it out like the nearby
Fishermen, propped on their wooden stools.

The girders rumble, the house lights opposite
Come on. Two dogfish have expired
In my landing-net. The madman
Has packed up his rod and tackle and gone.

RESTING UP

Every high-rise has a special feel to it.
My window opens out onto some of the few
Miserable mean tear-aways still left to sweat
The length of this big dipper,
But for me, no. In summer
I like to lie unbuttoned on my bed, and to
The tune of distant traffic I begin to scan
Page after page of any book I chance upon
In search of the shape of certain favourite words.
Nothing happens when I find them,
Maybe my lucky stars loosen up a little,
But it's hard to tell their shifted constellations
From the gentle flap of curtains in the cooling breeze.
I'll check for footprints in the sweet powdery dust
Banked along the window sill, and sprinkle bird-lime on
    the ledge outside,
Then evening falls – maybe I'll wake up one day
Covered in white fluff, and with a fat pigeon nesting on
    my feet!
'Lie back and think of anything'
I tell myself on these occasions, to relax my mind,
I need so much food, so much sleep, just so much sun
And exercise, to firm me up and improve my touch.

LEDGERS

Accordingly, I lay with my wife for three
Successive nights. During this exact period of time
The Mets beat the Cubs and it rained continuously.

October 8th. Fearful itching all over.
After much prodding and goading from H.
I agree to see a skin-specialist.

The park by starlight. The margins
Fill with doodles. This space, these
Pages, shelve ever more steeply into darkness . . .

OUTING

Ever since a willing spirit took me up
and began work on my reflexes, it feels
like I'm living the life my ancestors lived, though
I always imagine them as a wealthy jungle-dwelling
  people,
forever under the dripping elms.
If only it were truly impossible, and less like being a huge
  green amphibian
made to inch my home-sick coils between the different
  counters
of your favourite store, taking all these fancy cautions
to keep my head down, and out of other shoppers' way.
Your ankles I can just make out. The cash till rings,
though I'll never know what you at last decided on
out of so vast a choice of things, quite naturally
you refused to wait until the crush thinned out.
The dusty floor is cool, like a fountain,
worn smooth and comfortable by so many feet.
The trusty bell-boy follows obediently in your wake . . .
Now as I glide towards the whirr of sliding doors, I half-
  hope
its electric eye won't respond to my irregular approach.
  Another
spanking clean threshold! 'Open Sesame,' it cries, 'Hold
  tight!'
in its familiar Southern drawl, 'You know me well,
I won't be going to go to Hell for anybody.'